Written by Caroline Rowlands
Illustrations by Chris Dickason

Every effort has been made to ensure the accuracy of the
information in the first edition of this book, published in 2024.

First published in Great Britain in 2024 by Red Shed, part of Farshore

An imprint of HarperCollins*Publishers*
1 London Bridge Street, London SE1 9GF
www.farshore.co.uk

HarperCollins*Publishers*
Macken House, 39/40 Mayor Street Upper,
Dublin 1, D01 C9W8, Ireland

Red Shed is a registered trademark of HarperCollins*Publishers* Ltd.

Copyright © HarperCollins*Publishers* Limited 2024
Cover typography based on designs by Thy Bui
Illustration on page 59 by Emiliano Migliardo

ISBN 978 0 00 8660666 6

24 25 26 27 28 LBC 6 5 4 3 2
Printed in the United States of America

A CIP catalogue record for this title is available from the British Library.

Stay safe online. Any website addresses listed in this book are correct at the time of going to
print. However, Farshore is not responsible for content hosted by third parties. Please be aware
that online content can be subject to change and websites can contain content that is
unsuitable for children. We advise that all children are supervised when using the internet.

AMAZING FACTS

OLYMPICS & PARALYMPICS

RED SHED

Did you know?

Tug of war was once an Olympic sport.

Usain Bolt ate about 1,000 chicken nuggets during the 2008 Beijing Games.

The first Paralympics was held in Rome, Italy, in 1960.

The Winter Olympic torch was taken to space in 2014.

HB 04.05.2024 0829

Read on to discover over 100 fascinating and surprising facts about the world's biggest international sporting competitions and the incredible athletes who compete in them ...

The ancient Olympic Games took place a very, very long time ago . . . way back in 776BCE, to celebrate the Greek god Zeus.

Events included wrestling, long jump and chariot racing – most of the competitors took part naked!

CENSORED!

There are many rules to keep the Olympics fair and safe. But in Pankration, an ancient Greek combination of boxing and wrestling, the only rules were no biting or eye poking!

Anyone who made a false start (set off before everyone else) in an ancient Olympic race would be beaten with a stick.

Brutal punishments were given for any kind of cheating, including putting curses on other competitors – but that didn't stop some athletes from trying.

Ancient Olympic winners won an olive-leaf crown but there were no prizes for runners-up.

Winners were also rewarded with a statue of themselves in Olympia, where the Games took place, and if they won three times they got their picture painted. Some winners were also given free theatre tickets for life.

Emperor Theodosius I banned the Games in the fourth century, putting an end to the Olympics for 1,500 years.

But in 1896, after being inspired by the ancient Olympics, Frenchman Pierre de Coubertin founded the modern Olympics.

Only 14 nations competed in the first modern Summer Olympics in 1896.

Teams from 11 European countries joined teams from Australia, Chile and the USA at the first host city, Athens, Greece. Now more than 200 countries compete!

James Connolly was the first modern Olympic champion.

Not only did the American athlete win the triple jump in 1896, but he also finished second in the high jump and third in the long jump.

From 1912 to 1948, you could win an Olympic medal for painting, writing, sculpting, music and architecture!

In 1912, Walter Winans from the USA won a gold medal for sculpting a bronze horse pulling a chariot. He also won medals for shooting – a gold in 1908, and a silver in 1912.

Giving a poodle a haircut used to be an Olympic sport . . . or was it?

In the lead up to the 2008 Beijing Olympics, *The Telegraph* newspaper pranked readers on April Fool's Day (1st April) with an article about a supposed one-off poodle clipping event at the 1900 Paris Games.

The 1904 Summer Olympics were the first where gold, silver and bronze medals were awarded.

American gymnast George Eyser, who wore a wooden prosthetic leg, impressed everyone by winning six medals, three of them gold.

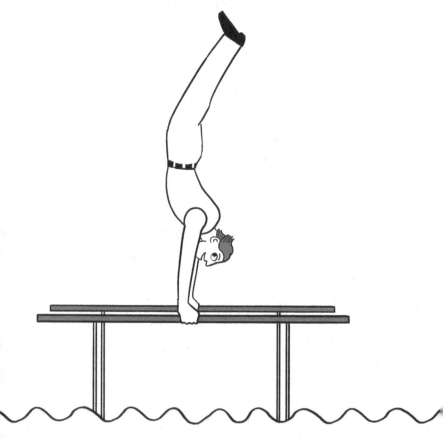

The first Olympic Village was built for the 1924 Summer Olympics in Paris.

A village to house all those taking part in the Games has been built for every Olympics ever since.

Tarzan was an Olympian!

Johnny Weissmuller, who played Tarzan in 12 movies, competed in the Olympics in the 1920s and won five gold medals in swimming events. He also won a bronze medal in water polo. What a CHIMPion!

Darth Vader was an Olympic fencer!

Well, an actor who played him was . . .
Bob Anderson, who was a body double for
the lightsaber fights in *Return of the Jedi* and
The Empire Strikes Back, competed in a team
fencing event in the 1952 Summer Olympics.

Women were not allowed to compete in the ancient Olympics, but Kyniska, the daughter of a Spartan king, managed to claim two Olympic victories in 396BCE and 392BCE.

Women were not even allowed to watch the Games, but they could own a chariot, so Kyniska snuck into the race with hers and became the first female Olympic champion!

It wasn't until the 1900 Summer Olympics in Paris that women were finally allowed to take part in the Games.

Only 22 of the 997 athletes that year were women, and they were only allowed to compete in five sports. Women competed against each other in golf and tennis, but competed against men in sailing, croquet and equestrian events.

At the 2012 Summer Olympics in London, every single Olympic sport had a men's and women's event.

Since 1991, there has been a rule that any new sport introduced to the Olympics must have a women's category as well as a men's.

Women's boxing was introduced at the London 2012 Games.

The first ever gold medals were won by Nicola Adams from Great Britain (flyweight), Katie Taylor from Ireland (lightweight) and Claressa Shields from the USA (middleweight).

German-Italian canoeist Josefa Idem competed in eight Olympics from 1984 to 2008 – the most Olympic appearances by a female athlete ever!

She represented two countries, West Germany in 1984 and then Italy from 1996, winning one gold, two silver and one bronze. Go, Josefa!

At the 2008 Beijing Games, Usain Bolt won the 100m, 200m and 4 x 100m relay events . . . and broke the world record in all three Olympic events!

Did you know that he also won gold in each of these events at the London 2012 and Rio 2016 Games? But it was the year after the Beijing Games when the Jamaican sprinter set the world record for the world's fastest 100m sprint (9.58 seconds) and became known as the fastest man in the world.

Usain Bolt ate around 1,000 McDonald's chicken nuggets during the 2008 Beijing Olympics.

The speedy sprinter ate at McDonald's most days in the Olympic Village and, luckily for him, all the food was free!

An Ethiopian runner won Olympic gold with bare feet.

After feeling uncomfortable in his trainers, Abebe Bikila decided to run the 1960 Olympic marathon in Rome, Italy, without them. He won gold once again at the 1964 Tokyo Olympics, but kept his trainers on this time!

The youngest female Olympic medal winner in an individual event was just 12 years and 21 days old!

Danish swimmer Inge Sørensen won bronze in the 200m breaststroke at the 1936 Summer Olympics in Berlin, Germany.

The youngest male Olympic medal winner in an individual event was Nils Skoglund.

The 14-year-old high diver from Sweden won silver at the 1920 Games in Antwerp, Belgium.

14-year-old Japanese swimmer Kusuo Kitamura is the youngest male Olympic gold medallist in an individual event.

He won the 1,500m freestyle gold at the Los Angeles Summer Games in 1932.

Marjorie Gestring from the US is the youngest Olympic gold medallist in an individual event.

She won the 3m springboard event at the 1936 Berlin Olympics when she was just 13 years and 268 days old. Even younger athletes have won medals in team events!

In 2021, Sky Brown became the youngest British competitor to win an Olympic medal.

Sky kick-flipped into history when she was just 13 years and 28 days old, winning a bronze medal for her skateboarding skills in Tokyo, Japan.

Eliza Pollock from the USA is the oldest female athlete to win an Olympic gold medal.

She was 63 years old when she won the archery competition at the 1904 Summer Olympics in St Louis, USA.

The oldest male Olympic winner was 72 years old!

Oscar Swahn from Sweden won Olympic gold in the 100m running deer double shot team event, at the 1920 Summer Olympics in Antwerp, Belgium. Competitors in this event shot at a moving deer-shaped target, winning points for how close they could get to small circles on the target.

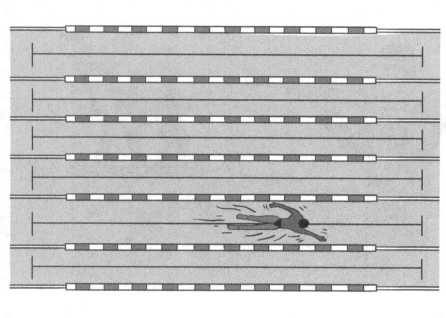

Eric Moussambani from Equatorial Guinea only learnt to swim a year before competing in the 2000 Sydney Olympics.

Eric hadn't ever swum in a 50m pool before. 17,000 people cheered him on as he finished his 100m freestyle heat, breaking the world record for the slowest swimming time. He still won – the other swimmers were disqualified for false starts!

Paralympic history began at a hospital for soldiers injured during World War II.

Dr Ludwig Guttman, who worked at a hospital in Stoke Mandeville, England, believed sports would help his patients. He organised some archery and netball competitions for them at the same time as the Summer Olympics were on in London in 1948.

The Paralympics itself began as the International Stoke Mandeville Games for wheelchair athletes in 1952.

A team of Dutch ex-soldiers competed alongside the British team, and these Games were held annually (every year).

By 1955, 18 countries were taking part.

Dr Ludwig Guttman hoped his Games for people with paraplegia (an inability to move their legs or lower body) would one day be thought of in the same way as the Olympic Games!

The first Paralympic Games took place in 1960 in Rome.

400 athletes from 23 nations competed in athletics, basketball, swimming, table tennis, archery, snooker, fencing and dartchery (a combination of darts and archery).

The Paralympic symbol has three elements and is also known as the Agitos (meaning 'I move').

Both the Olympic and Paralympic symbols use colours commonly found in national flags all over the world, but the Agitos also reflects the Paralympic motto – 'Spirit in Motion'!

One of the greatest ever British Paralympians, Tanni Grey-Thompson, won 16 Paralympic medals in wheelchair racing.

Competing in five Paralympic Games, from 1988 to 2004, Tanni won 11 gold medals, four silver and one bronze in the event.

Egyptian Paralympian Ibrahim Hamadtou holds the paddle in his mouth to play table tennis.

He lost both his arms when he was a child and serves the table tennis ball by throwing it into the air with his right foot.

Boccia and goalball are the only two sports in the Paralympics that aren't also part of the Olympic Games.

Boccia is thought to be one of the world's oldest games and involves a player throwing, kicking or using a ramp to push a ball towards a white marker ball.

David Smith won a Boccia gold for Great Britain at the 2016 Paralympics in Rio, Brazil.

In goalball – designed for players with visual impairments – two teams of three players compete to score points by bowling a ball along the floor and past the opposing side's goal line. All players wear blindfolds.

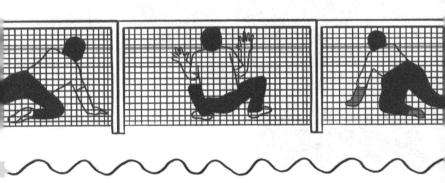

Poland's Natalia Partyka is the youngest athlete ever to take part in a Paralympic Games.

The table tennis player competed at her first Paralympics at just 11 years of age. Since then, Natalia has gone on to win five Paralympic gold medals!

Natalia Partyka and South African swimmer Natalie du Toit both competed in the 2008 Summer Olympics AND Paralympics in Beijing, China.

Natalia also carried the flag for her nation in both Games.

British swimmer Ellie Simmonds won gold in the 100m AND 400m freestyle races at the 2008 Beijing Paralympics, aged just 13.

Ellie also became the youngest winner of the BBC Young Sports Personality of the Year and the youngest recipient of an MBE (an award given to those who serve or honour their country) when she was 14.

Sarah Storey has won the most Paralympic gold medals for Great Britain – a whopping 17 in two different events.

She began her Paralympic career as a swimmer and won five gold medals in four Games. She then switched to cycling and pedalled her way to 12 more gold medals.

The first Winter Olympic Games took place in 1924 in Chamonix, France.

Around 250 athletes competed in events including ice-hockey, skating, curling and skiing. Norway was the most successful, with 17 medals.

Figure skating sensation Surya Bonaly performed an illegal backflip at the 1998 Winter Games in Nagano, Japan.

After falling over during her routine and realising she had no hope of winning, Surya entertained audiences with a backflip, landing on the blade of one skate. The judges deducted lots of points, as the move wasn't allowed, but the crowd loved it!

Walt Disney brought in more than 3,000 musicians, 2,000 birds and 30,000 balloons to entertain visitors and competitors at the 1960 USA Winter Olympics.

He also organised the opening and closing ceremonies, which were quite a spectacle and forever changed the way countries presented their own Olympic ceremonies.

From 1924 to 1992, the Winter and Summer Olympics took place in the same year, every four years.

This four-year period is called an Olympiad. The Summer and Winter Games are still held every four years, but since 1994, the Summer Olympics have been held during the first year of an Olympiad, and the Winter Olympics in the third year.

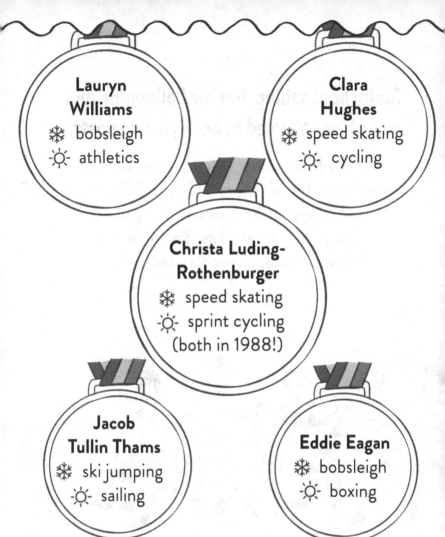

Lauryn Williams
❄ bobsleigh
☀ athletics

Clara Hughes
❄ speed skating
☀ cycling

Christa Luding-Rothenburger
❄ speed skating
☀ sprint cycling
(both in 1988!)

Jacob Tullin Thams
❄ ski jumping
☀ sailing

Eddie Eagan
❄ bobsleigh
☀ boxing

Only five athletes have won medals in both the Winter and Summer Olympics.

Motorboat sailing, hot-air ballooning and tug of war all used to be Olympic sports.

Each year, different sports and events are voted into (or out of) the Olympic Games. Some disappear then return, like golf and rugby, while others, like the swimming obstacle race, disappeared for ever.

Great Britain were the champions at tug of war!

The rope-pulling game was an Olympic sport from 1900 to 1920 and Great Britain won five medals, closely followed by the USA, who won three.

There was once an event called Plunge for Distance, where competitors dived into a pool to see how far they could drift underwater until they surfaced!

Five contestants, all from the USA, competed in this event at the 1904 Summer Olympics, and William Dickey took gold with a distance of almost 20m.

In 1912, athletes at the Stockholm Summer Games could compete for a medal by 'duelling' with guns.

Don't worry, they weren't allowed to fire their guns at each other! Instead, they had to shoot at dummies dressed in long coats, with a target painted on them.

The USA has more Olympic medals than any other country in the world!

With a huge haul of over 2,500 Olympic medals over the years, the USA has also won over 1,000 gold medals – the most gold medals won by a single nation.

Michael Phelps has won the most Olympic medals ever!

The US swimmer has competed in five Summer Olympic Games from 2000 to 2016, and 23 out of the 28 medals he won were gold!

Gold medals are mostly made of silver.

Yes, really! Gold medals used to be made from solid gold, but since 1912, silver has been used as a base material. The Olympic rules state that each medal must be made with at least 6g of gold. The value of the silver and gold in these gold medals is worth around £590.

In 1904, marathon runner Frederick Lorz became the first person to be disqualified from the Games!

Although he apparently crossed the finish line first, he actually was given a lift in his manager's car halfway around the course.

The Summer Olympic Games has been cancelled three times!

It was cancelled in 1916 due to World War I, then again in 1940 and 1944 because of World War II. In 2020 it was postponed because of the COVID-19 pandemic. The 2020 Tokyo Games finally went ahead in 2021 and were the first where nobody was allowed to cheer the athletes on in person.

The BBC televised the Summer Olympics for the first time in 1948, when it was held in London.

Twenty years later, in 1968, the broadcaster televised the Summer Olympics in Mexico City live in colour.

The Olympic torch is a modern invention that was inspired by the ancient Olympics.

The first torch relay was introduced in the 1936 Berlin Games. A few months before it started, the torch flame was lit in a curved mirror in Olympia, Greece. The flame was then passed from torch to torch in an international relay involving more than 3,000 athletes, until it reached Berlin.

The Winter Olympic torch travelled around the world and into space before reaching the 2014 Games in Sochi, Russia.

It travelled to the International Space Station aboard a Russian Soyuz rocket, blasting 418km into space at a speed of 28,164km/h.

Dina Asher-Smith is the fastest British woman in history!

The year before Dina made her Olympic debut at the Rio 2016 Games, she broke the national records for the 100m (10.83 seconds), 200m (21.88 seconds) and the team 4 x 100m races (41.77 seconds).

Mo Farah has four Olympic gold medals, the most of any British track athlete.

The talented runner won back-to-back golds in the 5,000m and 10,000m at the Summer Olympics in London 2012 and Rio 2016.

Olympic rower Steve Redgrave was the first British athlete to win five Olympic gold medals.

Cyclist Chris Hoy beat Steve's record after winning his sixth gold at the London 2012 Games. Then at Tokyo 2020, cyclist Jason Kenny became the most successful British Olympian ever by adding another gold to his collection – a total of seven!

Nadia Comăneci was the first Olympic gymnast to be awarded a perfect ten.

At the 1976 Summer Olympics in Montreal, Canada, 14-year-old Comăneci received seven perfect scores and won gold medals in three different events.

The scoreboard was not designed for such brilliance ... and had to record her perfect ten as '1.00'.

At the 2000 Summer Olympics in Sydney, Australia, officials set the gymnastics vault to the wrong height in error.

It wasn't until Australian gymnast Allana Slater questioned the vault's low height that it was measured and the mistake was revealed. The wrong height even caused gold-medal favourite Svetlana Khorkina to land on her bum!

The US men's basketball team refused to accept their silver medal at the 1972 Summer Olympics in Munich, Germany.

The US team thought the final whistle had been blown and celebrated a victory, only for extra seconds to be added to the game. Their opponents from the former Soviet Union managed to score and win Olympic gold instead.

The Winklevoss twins from the USA, who rowed in the 2008 Beijing Summer Olympics, are also famous for sueing the creator of Facebook.

Cameron and Tyler Winklevoss claimed Mark Zuckerberg stole their idea for the social media site and were eventually given $65 million (around £51 million) by the Facebook creator.

British 400m sprinter Derek Redmond was helped over the finish line at the 1992 Summer Olympics by his dad.

As Redmond sprinted around the track in Barcelona, Spain, he felt his hamstring tear. Ouch! He collapsed to the floor, but was determined to continue. His dad jumped over the barriers to help him finish the race – which got the biggest cheer of the entire Games.

At the 1936 Summer Olympics in Berlin, two Japanese pole vaulters created a new kind of Olympic medal.

Instead of going into a tie-breaker to decide who would win silver and who would win bronze, Shūhei Nishida and Sueo Ōe had their silver and bronze medals cut in half. The bronze was fused with the silver to make two new friendship medals.

Harold Sakata, who acted in the James Bond movie *Goldfinger* (1964), was also an Olympic silver medallist.

He won the medal for the USA at the 1948 Summer Olympics in London, and represented his country again during his later career as a professional wrestler.

Harold Abrahams was the first British (and European) runner to win an Olympic sprint title.

He won gold for the 100m at the 1924 Summer Games, and his win was so monumental that it was turned into an Oscar-winning film: *Chariots of Fire* (1981).

Over six million second-hand mobile phones, digital cameras, gaming devices and laptops were recycled to create the medals for the Tokyo 2020 Summer Olympics.

The devices were donated by the Japanese population, then taken apart and melted down to make more environmentally friendly medals.

Tennis was removed from the Summer Olympics in 1928 and didn't return as an event until 1988.

In 2012, Andy Murray became the first British man to win the Olympic singles gold medal in tennis since Josiah Ritchie in 1908.

Frank Kugler is the only athlete in Olympic history to win a medal in three different sports.

He won a silver medal in men's freestyle wrestling, two bronze medals in weightlifting, and another bronze in the team tug of war event at the 1904 Summer Olympics in St Louis, USA.

Pál Szekeres is the only athlete to have won medals at both the Olympic and Paralympic Games.

The Hungarian fencer won a bronze medal at the 1988 Summer Olympics. He was injured in a car accident, but didn't let this put an end to his success. He went on to win three gold and three bronze medals in five Paralympic Games.

Japanese wrestler Kaori Icho, US long jumper Carl Lewis, US discus thrower Alfred Oerter and Danish sailor Paul Elvstrøm have all won four Summer Olympic gold medals at four consecutive Games!

In team events, Hungarian fencer Aladár Gerevich won six Olympic gold medals at six consecutive Games.

US basketball player Lisa Leslie is another Olympic legend, having been part of four Olympic gold-medal-winning women's teams.

The first Winter Paralympics was held in 1976 in Örnsköldvik, Sweden.

Great Britain has competed in every Winter Paralympics, and in 1984, John Watkins and Peter Young won the nation's first Paralympic medals (both bronze).

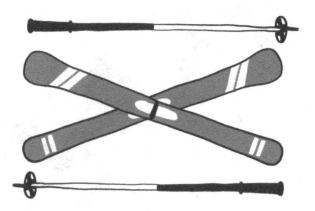

Bonnie St. John was the first Black woman to win a Winter Paralympic medal.

The alpine skier from Florida, USA, made history after winning a silver and two bronzes at the 1984 Winter Paralympics in Austria.

Trischa Zorn has won the most Paralympic medals ever!

The American has swum her way to 41 gold, nine silver and five bronze medals.

Team USA has won more Paralympic medals than any other nation.

The US team has been present for every Summer and Winter Paralympics since they began.

Team GB has a total of 2,000 Paralympic medals, and over 600 of them are gold.

Germany has won the most medals at the Winter Paralympics.

Prior to the Beijing 2008 Paralympics, elevators and wheelchair ramps were installed on the Great Wall of China.

Accessibility was also improved in popular tourist places like the Forbidden City and the Imperial Palace.

The Rio 2016 Summer Olympics saw 36 sets of siblings competing . . .

. . . including Andy and Jamie Murray in men's tennis, Serena and Venus Williams in women's tennis, Aria and Makenzie Fischer in water polo (their dad was an Olympic water polo player too!) and Rieko and Akira Ioane in rugby.

King Charles III's sister, Princess Anne, competed in the 1976 Summer Olympics.

The princess was part of the equestrian team and rode a horse called Goodwill, which belonged to her mother, Queen Elizabeth II. Princess Anne's daughter, Zara Tindall, competed in the same event at the 2012 London Summer Olympics and won a silver medal.

At the London 2012 Summer Olympics, British brothers Alistair and Jonny Brownlee took first and third place in the men's triathlon.

Four years later, Alistair retained his Olympic title and won gold again, while Jonny came second.

Leila, Liina and Lily Luik from Estonia were the first triplets to compete against each other at an Olympic Games.

They made history when they all took part in the Olympic marathon in Rio 2016.

Kenyan-born long-distance runner Bernard Lagat is a five-time Olympian, having competed in the 2000, 2004, 2008, 2012 and 2016 Games.

In 2016, he was joined at the Summer Olympics in Rio by his sister, Viola Cheptoo, who is a middle-distance runner.

At the 1988 Winter Olympics, four brothers made up both of Mexico's two-person bobsleigh teams.

Eduardo, Jorge, Adrian and Roberto Tames hold the Guinness World Record for the most siblings to compete in a single Winter Olympics event.

All four brothers were also part of the 1992 Winter Olympics squad.

Roberto and Jorge competed on separate teams in the two-person bobsleigh, while Adrian was in the four-person team with Eduardo as a reserve.

The tradition of starting Olympic races with a pistol dates back to cowboy races in the early 19th century.

Since the 1948 Summer Olympics, starter pistols have been attached to an electronic system that projects a beam of light across the finish line and shows how long an athlete took to finish a race.

The ancient Greeks began their races with a system of ropes.

One cord was pulled across the ancient Olympic starting line at waist-level and another at the knees; when the cords were dropped, the race began.

Olympic athletes do not get paid for participating in the Olympic Games.

However, in some nations an athlete who wins a medal gets a cash bonus!

Some countries, like the UK, give all their athletes money to pay for their coaches and training venues instead.

British Olympic and Paralympic athletes competing in the Paris 2024 Summer Games received £232 million in funding.

Jonnie Peacock not only won gold in the 100m at the 2012 and 2016 Paralympic Games, but he was also the first amputee to boogie on down on *Strictly Come Dancing*.

When Jonnie was just five years old, an illness caused him to have his right leg amputated below the knee. Jonnie dreamt of being a footballer but went on to become a world-class sprinter.

Stadium Australia in Sydney is the largest stadium to have hosted an Olympic Games so far.

114,714 people were at the closing ceremony in 2000 – the largest crowd ever to attend an Olympic event.

In 1956, the Summer Olympics was held in two different cities on two different continents.

Melbourne, Australia, was picked as the host city, but because of very strict laws about allowing horses into the country, all the equestrian events were held in Stockholm, Sweden.

Only five sports have appeared at every Olympics since 1896.

These are athletics, cycling, fencing, swimming and gymnastics.

At the Paris 2024 Summer Games, around 10,500 athletes from 206 nations will compete.

32 sports will be featured, with a total of 329 events.

Look out for other books in the series!

AMAZING FACTS
KING CHARLES III

AMAZING FACTS
SIR DAVID ATTENBOROUGH

AMAZING GROSS FACTS
EVERY 6 YEAR OLD NEEDS TO KNOW

AMAZING GROSS FACTS
EVERY 7 YEAR OLD NEEDS TO KNOW

AMAZING GROSS FACTS
EVERY 8 YEAR OLD NEEDS TO KNOW

AMAZING GROSS FACTS
EVERY 9 YEAR OLD NEEDS TO KNOW

AMAZING GROSS FACTS
EVERY 10 YEAR OLD NEEDS TO KNOW

AMAZING PUZZLES & QUIZZES
FOR EVERY 6 YEAR OLD

AMAZING PUZZLES & QUIZZES
FOR EVERY 7 YEAR OLD

AMAZING PUZZLES & QUIZZES
FOR EVERY 8 YEAR OLD

AMAZING PUZZLES & QUIZZES
FOR EVERY 9 YEAR OLD

AMAZING PUZZLES & QUIZZES
FOR EVERY 10 YEAR OLD

AMAZING PUZZLES & QUIZZES
EASTER

The Paris Games is introducing breaking (or breakdancing) as a new event.

32 athletes will compete for a medal with their best toprocks, downrocks, power moves and freezes. A sporting event guaranteed to turn heads!